This book belongs to

_____

This book is dedicated to my children - Mikey, Kobe, and Jojo.
Focus is like a muscle you have to train regularly so it performs optimally.

Focused Ninja

By Mary Nhin

Pictures by
Jelena Stupar

"All done!" exclaimed Focused Ninja as he closed his book.

Focused Ninja finished his math homework and read the two chapters his teacher assigned.

He was able to maintain his focus while his siblings practiced their instruments and his mother baked banana bread.

Whenever Focused Ninja had a task to do, or if he set his mind on accomplishing something, he had a remarkable way of staying focused until it was complete.

Focused Ninja could maintain his concentration in all sorts of situations.

During school, when his teacher was talking, he sat in the front so he could listen intently and take notes.

At school and at home, Focused Ninja liked to keep his desk and room tidy so he could focus and easily find things when he needed them.

And when he had a big job to complete, he split the assignment into "bite-size" tasks so he wouldn't feel overwhelmed.

But Focused Ninja didn't always have this wonderful capacity to concentrate.

Once upon a time, he could lose his attention quite easily.

When his mother asked him to clean his room, he would often have trouble following directions.

While listening during story time, he would fidget, talk, and get up.

And if he was pouring cereal into a bowl, he wouldn't be able to slow down enough to do it carefully without spilling it.

Until one day his friend, Confident Ninja, showed him how he could increase his focus.

You can use any or all of these tools:

Find distractions and eliminate them.

Organize.

Choose greens and healthy foods.

Use exercise to give your brain a boost.

Split up large assignments into smaller tasks.

When Focused Ninja went to school the next day, he made different choices and it made all the difference:

Find distractions and eliminate them.

He found that other kids' talking distracted him, so he chose to sit in the front, even though he was shy.

Organize.

He never before thought about tidying his desk but today was different.

Today, was the day it all changed. He organized his desk.

Choose to eat greens and healthy foods.

At lunch, he chose to eat a healthy lunch with vegetables.

Use exercise to give your brain a boost.

And then at recess, he used exercise to give his brain a boost.

Split up large assignments into smaller tasks.

When he got home to work on his homework, he split up the big assignment into smaller tasks.

Focused Ninja was able to focus more than just that one day.

He continued to use these strategies found in the F.O.C.U.S. method every day in his life. Soon, he was known as the most focused ninja of all.

Remembering the F.O.C.U.S. method could be your secret weapon against a lack of focus.

Check out our Ninja Life Journal on Amazon
or visit us at growgrit.co

 @marynhin @GrowGrit
#NinjaLifeHacks

 Mary Nhin Grow Grit

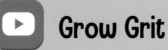 Grow Grit